How to Create
MULTIGENERATIONAL
WEALTH

by

S. Brooks Wicker, Jr. CPA

ISBN: 1501077937
ISBN 13: 9781501077937
Library of Congress Control Number: 2014915986
CreateSpace Independent Publishing Platform,
North Charleston, South Carolina

TABLE OF CONTENTS

Chapter 1

THE THREE PILLARS OF WEALTH CREATION^{SM}

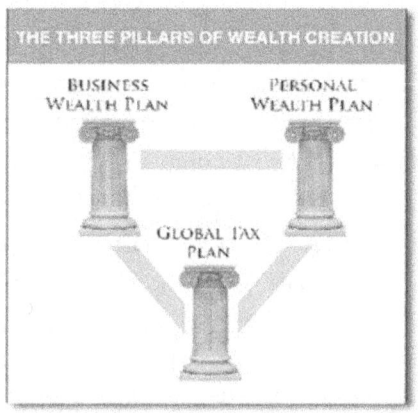

There are many obstacles to creating multigenerational wealth. Some are large and difficult and seemingly beyond our control. Most are much simpler and just require us to pay attention to detail and to be aware. But overcoming all the challenges to creating wealth requires complex planning. Few of us are able to overcome these obstacles alone.

This book is a guide for anyone to overcoming and mastering these hindrances and truly creating his or her own multigenerational wealth.

The following will sound familiar to most of us.

Sam is on his way out of town to meet with one of his favorite clients. He has a pleasant day of golf planned and he is also hoping to ink a new project while on the course. It's a beautiful day and life is good.

While Sam is driving, his cell phone buzzes and he notices it is his banker. He has been working with her for a couple of months to arrange a new line of credit for the expansion of his business into a new market.

Sam answers his phone and the conversation goes something like this:

"Hello, this is Sam."

"Sam, this is Nancy. I finally got a hearing with the loan committee tomorrow morning. I need you to send over the most current financials you can. What I have on file is now six months old and I know that will be the first issue I will have to overcome. You know how hard it has been to get in front of the committee. I don't want to have to put this off, or risk them turning your request down because we don't have current information. We may not get another hearing for at least a month."

Sam thinks: Great. My CPA is on vacation and Cindy, my head bookkeeper, has not been performing very well of late. As a matter of fact, the information she gives him internally never looks anything like what he gets from his CPA firm at year end, which he always gets too late to be of much benefit in running the business.

He has very little confidence in the information Cindy provides. But what is he going to do? Cindy has been with him for 10 years. He knows he has outgrown Cindy's capabilities. Sam is no longer a one man show.

"OK, Nancy, I am traveling out of town today. I will call the office and get something over to you right away."

Sam hangs up with Nancy and calls his office only to find that Cindy didn't come in today. Her daughter is sick and home from school. That kid is always sick! Then he starts to wonder: "How much is that costing the firm in insurance premiums when we renew? The rate went up 20% last year."

His next thought is, "OK, who can I call at Jim's CPA firm to get this done?" He realizes that there isn't anyone. Jim is on vacation and the junior who always worked on his account just took a new job. Besides, any information they have is six months old and there is no way he is going to get any information out of them today. He also has been handling all of the negotiations with the bank himself and would have to bring them up to speed.

While he is thinking of what to do his phone buzzes again. It's his wife Sara. She is calling to remind him of his daughter Katie's play this evening. Oh great, he will have to miss it. This is the third family event he has missed in the last couple of months. He barely made his son's birthday last month.

He explains the situation to his wife. Needless to say, she is not happy.

Once again his phone buzzes. It's Bud, Sam's financial advisor. Bud is an old college buddy and has been handling his personal portfolio and the retirement and benefit planning for his business. Sam has not been happy with Bud for a while. Bud never seems to have any input on how he is doing other than, we got a return of x% but if he moved to this latest greatest product that did xx% last year he might make more. Bud does not appear to understand his business at all or even show any interest in it. There doesn't appear to be any coordination between what he is doing personally and what he is doing at his company. He has also noticed that he appears to be paying a ton of taxes on his investments for the past couple of years.

Worse, Bud and Jim never talk and coordinate anything, unless of course Sam gets them in the same room. And then he does not understand what they are talking about. He quit doing this a few years ago because nothing ever came of the meetings anyway. Bud never had any new ideas except for the latest greatest product, and

Jim was only concerned about what happened last year and nothing was coordinated any better than before. On top of that it usually cost him a chunk of money; they are all friends so the three of them usually met at the golf course, along with Sam's attorney Bill to round out a foursome. Bill even charged him for his time the last time they all got together, and never contributed much to the financial conversation anyway except to offer to review his estate and to draw up some trusts that he did not understand.

So of course he did nothing.

Well, now Sam's beautiful day is ruined. He has no choice but to call his client and cancel the day. Sam has to return to the office and handle everything.

Again!

Sound familiar?

If you are like most of my clients, you answered a resounding "YES!"

"Stuff like this drives me crazy!"

When I ask my business owner clients, "How much of your day is made up of dealing with this type of distraction?" I get answers that range from "half of my day" to "that's all I do. Business is no fun anymore."

"There has to be a better way!"

Well, there is. Read on and learn how to free yourself from all or most of these distractions. How to get all aspects of your financial life working together in a coordinated way that will maximize your wealth while lessening your tax burden. In other words, you can create more wealth and keep more of what you create.

I realize that not everyone reading this book will be a business owner. Fear not. If you are an upper-level executive or sales executive with a high income, we have the answer for you as well. I have an entire chapter devoted to you and your concerns. You have the same issues on the personal and tax side as the business owner just without the additional headaches that go with owning a business.

Many of you may have those headaches as well. You just do not own the business. You run it, either because it is closely owned by a family group or it is a publicly traded company.

In the following chapters we will discuss the three pillars of wealth creation[SM];

Chapter 2: The Business Wealth Plan (for business owners. Those of you who do not own or run a business can feel free to skip this chapter, although it has some great information that you may find beneficial).

Chapter 3: The Personal Wealth Plan

Chapter 4: Tying it All Together – the global tax plan

It may be helpful to define what a wealth plan is before we go any further as the wealth plan is the bedrock of multigenerational wealth creation.

Some of you are probably thinking "I know what that is. I had a broker with one of the big warehouses produce a plan for me a few years ago. He charged me $10,000 and gave me a bound document that we never fully implemented, primarily because it appeared to benefit him more than me. Besides, he didn't follow up and I don't have time to chase him around for answers. And he pretty much completely disappeared during the market downturn when his plan lost me a good portion of my portfolio."

No, a wealth plan is not the typical "financial plan" most of us know about. A wealth plan is far more comprehensive and actually includes 2 to 3 comprehensive plans (depending on if you own a business). You will not see these comprehensive plans offered by warehouses, CPA firms, law firms, banks or other financial institutions. Wealth plans require all of these services or the coordination of all of these services. Think about it: when was the last time your financial advisor looked at your tax returns or your CPA reviewed your investment plan, or your lawyer looked at either, not to mention what your banker or insurance agent looked at? Would any of them know and fully understand what they were looking at and how they were interrelated and dependent on each other, how much one affected the results of the other?

I bet the answer is they have never reviewed these other plans or at least not in years and no I don't think they would understand how critical it is that they work together efficiently!

Wealth Plans are the province of the Super Rich. They are how the Super Rich stay that way.

Chapter 2

THE BUSINESS WEALTH PLAN

'll bet no one has ever talked to you about a Business Wealth Plan. We all have heard of the business plan, the marketing plan, etc. And there are all kinds of people out there who want to sell you one of these plans, only to have it relegated to a shelf in your office and never really thought of again.

These are all just a part of a business wealth plan.

Let's start at the beginning: why did you start your business (or why did your grandfather or your dad or your mom) in the first place? It is usually for one of two reasons:

1. To have a job, to pay the mortgage and put food on the table and to be able to do it on your own terms.
2. To create a valuable asset that you could sell or pass along to your heirs. In other words, to create multigenerational wealth.

Quite frankly, most people start a business for the first reason. And there is nothing wrong with that. You can still become very comfortable financially with proper planning. That doesn't mean, however, that you can't change your focus and begin to build true wealth.

The Business Wealth Plan Process

Determine your target

The first step to building the business wealth plan is like on any journey, to decide where you want to go. As Dr. Steven Covey (*The 7 Habits of Highly Effective People*) says, "Start with the end in mind."

How much do you want your business to be worth and when do you want to reach that target? What will your business look like when you arrive at your goal?

Determine your starting point

The next step is to determine where you are now. Now that we know what you want your business to look like, what you want it to be worth and when you want to reach that goal, we can better determine where you are now on your journey to your goal.

Coordinate with your Global Tax Plan

I will say this several times throughout this book; **Taxes are the greatest detriment to wealth accumulation that exists!**

We will discuss the Global Tax Plan in greater detail in chapter 4.

Develop your plan and establish benchmarks

The third step is to determine the actions that are most likely to get you to your goal. It is important to have definite goals with dates for achieving those goals, like one year goals, 3 year goals, 5 year goals and so on. You must be diligent in measuring how well you are doing on each of those goals. There is an old saying: "you can only control what you can measure".

Now you can finally begin developing the Business Plan, Marketing Plan, etc.

Implement your plan

This is where most professional relationships fall short. It does no good to develop a plan, no matter how comprehensive and well thought out, if it is never fully implemented.

Most consultants create very impressive documents that they deliver at the end of their engagement. That's the problem, most consultants or advisors view their work as done when they deliver the plan or perhaps sell you a few products.

Any engagement should include the full implementation of the agreed upon plan and the next and final step.

Monitor progress toward your benchmarks and adjust as needed.

I recommend that you meet with your contract CFO monthly or quarterly at the very least.

As the old saying goes "Man plans and God laughs." Again, no matter how comprehensive and well thought out your plan, it is imperative that you and your contract CFO monitor your progress and meet to adjust the plan and/or your benchmarks as situations change. Just the process of implementation and monitoring will uncover areas that need to be tweaked. Remember you can only control what you can measure. That is what these meetings are for measuring results, getting an unbiased professional read on your progress, adjusting the plan for life events, and keeping you focused.

Ok, now we know what a business wealth plan is. How do you leverage that to create multigenerational wealth?

Remember Sam from chapter one? The harried business owner who had to cancel his day of golf with his favorite client and possibly lose out on a new project because of it?

Sam decided there had to be a better way. He decided to develop a wealth plan for his business and to hire a contract CFO to help him create and monitor the plan so he could stay on course. (His contract CFO is also his personal CFO. More on that in chapter 3.)

As part of his wealth planning, he explored what was the best and highest use of his time in achieving his goals for the business. Not surprisingly, what he discovered was that canceling the golf date with one of his best clients so he could go back to the office and clean up everything that was not functioning was not the best use of his time. Not only did he miss out on the relaxing golf day, he did not make any money that day and he missed out on the opportunity to close some new business costing him thousands of dollars in revenue. On top of that, he also paid Cindy for a full day's work that she did not perform.

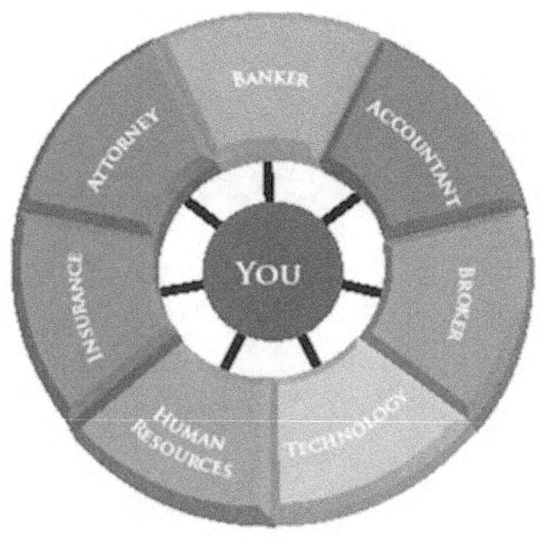

ILLUSTRATION 1

Typical Business Arrangement

Sam had reached the classic point in most businesses when they have grown to a certain point. Sam was the guy in the middle (illustration 1). He was answering to all of the external vendors and the internal vendors. As we discussed in chapter one, business owners in Sam's position feel that they spend one half to most of their time dealing with all of these distractions - not exactly the best use of his time in executing his business wealth plan.

So what's the solution, you ask.

The solution has historically been the rarefied grounds of the Super Rich and has historically not been applied in the business world. In the world of the Super Rich, it is called the Family Office which is basically outsourcing all functions you can to professionals who are more efficient, more accurate and typically less expensive than having in house employees. (Illustration 2)

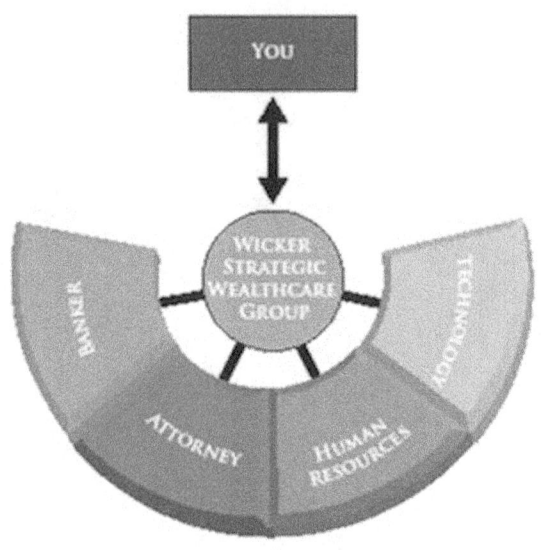

ILLUSTRATION 2

Optimal Business Arrangement

As you can see from this illustration, the idea is to take Sam out of the middle and reduce his distractions/contact point to one person or group. Taking this simple step can give Sam back one half to most of his day to spend any way he wants.

Since Sam has outsourced his entire accounting and finance departments and he now has a contract CFO, getting financials to the bank while he is out of town is no longer a problem. Another benefit is that the financials for Sam's company are available to him 24/7 from practically anywhere in the world, and they are always accurate and up to date. This also saves a great deal on the cost of tax compliance and planning at tax time since the contract CFO firm to whom Sam outsourced his accounting and finance departments also prepares both his company and his personal taxes.

Sam's contract CFO also coordinates with his banker and attorney. The contract CFO in addition to being a CPA is also a licensed securities representative, a registered advisory agent and holds licenses in life and health insurance so he is also handling both his business and his personal investment and risk management plans. His contract CFO also has relationships with HR and IT professionals and coordinates those activities for Sam's business as well.

In addition to having access to his company books 24/7, Sam also has access to all of his bank accounts, both personal and business; his portfolios, personal and 401(k); his tax returns, personal and business; his wealth plans, business and personal; his estate plan; his global tax plan; and his insurance policies. He is in complete control of all of this with nothing more than a smart phone. He never has to wait for an answer or for a document.

Sam's time is now his own. He can spend more time growing the business. He can make his daughter's plays and his sons hockey games.

When he goes on vacation, he is not constantly worried about what is going on and making calls to check on things.

Sam now meets monthly, more frequently if necessary, with his contract CFO (again the same firm who he has outsourced his other services to) to discuss progress on the business wealth plan and evaluate where they are on the journey so corrections can be made as necessary. Sam now feels comfortable that he is maximizing the value of his number one asset, his business. He is maximizing his return from the business while minimizing his tax burden and consequently he is maximizing his overall wealth. Sam's business has grown substantially over the past couple of years and he is finally seeing the results of the leverage points his contract CFO taught him about on the bottom line. Sam is enjoying business again.

He has peace of mind that everything is working smoothly, efficiently and cost effectively and he is on top of what is going on because he has just one contact point who provides or coordinates all of his financial needs.

For the business owner, it all boils down to this. Your business is the most valuable asset you own. The funds to do everything on the personal side of the ledger flow from your business. It is essential that we maximize the profitability and value of your business, while minimizing your tax burden (the subject of chapter 4) if you have any hope of creating multigenerational wealth. If we don't get this right, the rest is just window dressing.

Of course this must be fully coordinated with your personal wealth plan (chapter 3) and your global tax plan (chapter 4) to be effective.

THE PERSONAL WEALTH PLAN

In chapter one we defined what a wealth plan is. It is more than a standard financial plan in that it encompasses your estate plan, your investment plan, your retirement plan (including your 401(k), stock options, deferred compensation and other plans you have at work), and your giving plan and it is coordinated with your global tax plan (more on this in chapter 4).

Just like with the business wealth plan, we start with where you want to go. This is not just your target retirement date but also the size of the estate you want to leave, what you want to do with that estate, and who you want to provide for. We must develop a picture in your mind that you can instantly recall. This is where you dream big, but to be realistic, we usually ask that you come up with three levels: Your wildest dreams, Your wouldn't it be great dream, and Your I have arrived dream.

I will now discuss the elements of the Personal Wealth Plan. These elements are virtually the same as for the Business Wealth Plan so if you read chapter one you may want to skip ahead. If not read on, it is critical that you understand the process of wealth planning.

The Personal Wealth Plan Process

Determine your target

The first step to building your wealth plan is like on any journey, to decide where you want to go. As Dr. Steven Covey (*The 7 Habits of Highly Effective People*) says, "Start with the end in mind."

Determine your starting point

The next step is to determine where you are now. Now that we know where you want to go, what you want your estate to be worth and when you want to reach that goal, we can better determine where you are now on your journey to your goal.

The important thing to remember is there are as many ways to accomplish this as there are people on earth. There is no one magic bullet that is right for everyone. There is no one product or product provider that works for all situations.

Coordinate with your Global Tax Plan

I will say this several times throughout this book; **Taxes are the greatest detriment to wealth accumulation that exists!**

We will discuss the Global Tax Plan in greater detail in chapter 4.

Develop your plan and establish benchmarks

The fourth step is to determine the actions that are most likely to get you to your goal. It is important to have definite goals with dates for achieving those goals, like one year goals, 3 year goals, 5 year goals and so on. You must be diligent in measuring how well you are doing on each of those goals. There is an old saying: "you can only control what you can measure".

We will also assess where you are currently, your risk profile, and your risk exposure. From this we determine the best path to get you to your goal.

Implement your plan

This is where most professional relationships fall short. It does no good to develop a plan, no matter how comprehensive and well thought out if it is never fully implemented.

Most consultants create very impressive documents that they deliver at the end of their engagement. That's the problem, most consultants or advisors view their work as done when they deliver the plan or perhaps sell you a few products.

Any engagement should include the full implementation of the agreed upon plan and the next and final step.

Monitor progress toward benchmarks and adjust as needed.

I recommend that you meet with your personal CFO monthly or quarterly at the very least (meeting with your personal CFO can be reduced to quarterly once your plans are implemented and you fully understand the benchmarks and how to monitor them).

As the old saying goes "Man plans and God laughs." Again, no matter how comprehensive and well thought out your plan, it is imperative that you and your contract/personal CFO monitor your progress and meet to adjust the plan and/or your benchmarks as situations change. Just the process of implementation and monitoring will uncover areas that need to be tweaked. Remember you can only control what you can measure. That is what these meetings are for; measuring results, getting an unbiased professional read on your progress, adjusting the plan for life events, and keeping you focused.

This is complex stuff. This is not what you do every day. Consequently you are very ill equipped to take care of this yourself. As the old adage goes, you would not take out your own appendix, would you? No, you would go to an expert, or actually a team of experts working together.

You, like the business owner we discussed in the previous chapter, are the one in the middle. (Reprint illustration 1)

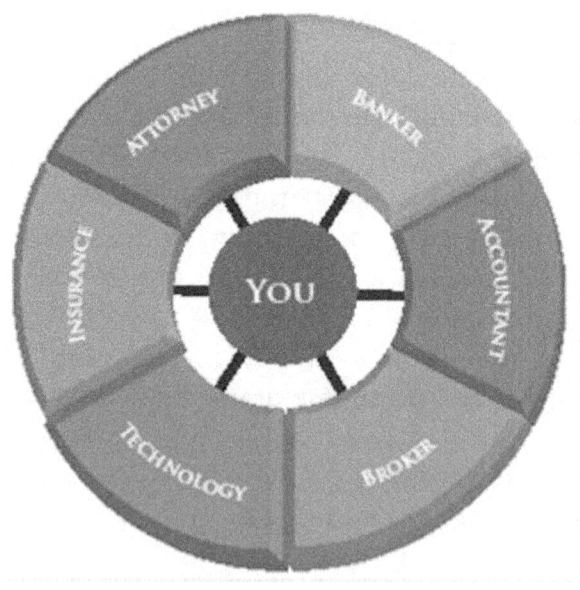

ILLUSTRATION 1

Typical Personal Arrangement

You have fewer external vendors than the business owner but each one is just as critical to your success. Just like the business owner, you do not hear from these vendors unless they are selling something. They do not talk to each other unless you ask them to and when they do they do not speak the same language. Typically you end up more confused than when you started and you either do nothing or the wrong thing.

You need to take a page out of the play book of the Super Rich. You need a personal CFO. (Reprint illustration 2).

ILLUSTRATION 2

Optimal Personal Arrangement

A personal CFO deals in all of these confusing issues every day. He speaks the language of all of your external vendors and he either provides or coordinates most of the services and products required to meet your goals. He literally takes you out of the middle.

Moreover you will have quarterly meetings (more frequent if needed) to monitor your progress toward your goals. Just as with the business owner, you will have 24/7 access to all of your bank and investment accounts, your tax returns, your insurance policies, your estate plan, your mortgage information, travel itineraries, credit card information and any other information you want to have accessible at all times. This can all be accessed via computer, smart phone or tablet from virtually anywhere in the world.

In between these quarterly meetings, you can communicate via phone, or web conference while you and your contract CFO both view any related documents.

As mentioned previously this is all coordinated with your global tax plan, the subject of chapter 4.

Remember Sam from chapter one? He utilizes a contract CFO for his business as well a personal CFO. Not only did he outsource his accounting and financials for his business, he did the same personally. Sam's contact point is the same for both his business finances and his personal finances. He is experiencing greater efficiencies and savings now that his business plan, personal plan and tax plan are all coordinated.

In his case, the same professional serves both the contract CFO and personal CFO roles. This is usually the case but not always. Some clients will utilize a team approach where the personal CFO is the lead on the team. The team should also be from the same firm to insure continuity and efficiency in both services and cost.

Sam is enjoying his business more and is less stressed now that he has the confidence that he is progressing toward his business and personal goals. He knows that all aspects of his financial life are in good hands and that they are being monitored by professionals, something he certainly cannot claim to be.

He is experiencing growth in his business even while he is working less. Now that there is coordination between his Business and Personal Plans he is seeing increased planned growth in his net worth.

And best of all, he is keeping more of the wealth he is creating because his wealth plans are truly coordinated with his global tax plan.

Chapter 4

THE GLOBAL TAX PLAN

Taxation is the greatest detriment to the creation of wealth that exists today!

Taxpayers in the upper tax brackets experienced huge increases in their income taxes for the 2013 tax year. And I hate to be the bearer of bad news but, **it is only going to get worse!**

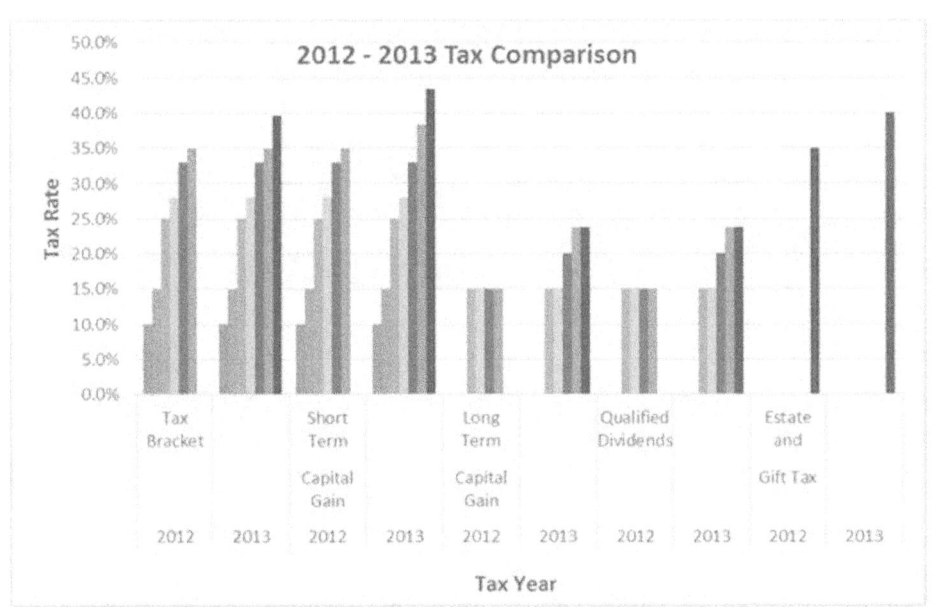

As the previous chart above demonstrates, tax rates under the American Tax Relief Act of 2012 have increased substantially.

Guess where the taxes are going to come from? You got it: those Americans (actually worldwide) in the upper tax brackets. A great deal will also come from stealth taxes on the middle class but the lions share will come from taxpayers in the upper brackets.

If you have taxable income of $400,000 or more, it is now more important than ever that where you invest your money offers the opportunity for tax deferral. Investment location is as important as investment allocation. With record low interest rates and markets reaching new highs, it is also critical that you put a portion of your investable assets in vehicles that are not affected by volatility.

After all, what you keep is more important than what you make (see the table on the following page). This is true not only for return but also for the value of your estate.

Cost of loss in a $100,000 portfolio

Market declines 10% - portfolio declines to $90,000

How much do you have to earn to get back to your original investment?

10,000/90,000= 11.11%

Market decline of 20% - portfolio declines to $80,000

Amount need to recover loss: 20,000/80,000= 25%

Market declines 25% - portfolio declines to $75,000

Amount need to recover loss: 25,000/75,000=33.33%

Actual return on a $100,000 portf0lio at 39.5% tax bracket*

10% return on $100,000 = $10,000

After tax return $10,000x60.5%= $6,050

Actual return = 6.05%

tax reduction in return 3.95%

15% return on $100,000 portfolio = $15,000

After tax return $15,000x60.5%= $9,075

Actual return = 9.075%

tax reduction in return 5.925%

20% return on $100,000 portfolio = $20,000

After tax return = $20,000 x 60.5%= $12,100

Actual return = 12.1%

tax reduction in return 7.9%

*Does not consider state or local taxes which can bring your true tax rate up to over 50% in many locations.

As you can see the greater the loss, the higher the return you must earn to get back to even. Also, the greater the return percentage, the bigger the decrease in true after-tax return.

If you are a business owner, entity selection is more critical than ever. Under the new tax law there is a new 3.8% tax on net investment income. Income derived from a partnership is included in net investment income while income derived from a Subchapter

S Corporation is not. Likewise, income from a Partnership or LLC taxed as a partnership is subject to expanded self-employment tax and expanded Medicare tax.

Now is the time to review the taxable entity for your business.

As I asked before, when was the last time your financial advisor looked at your tax returns? If he did, did he know what he was looking at? Did he have recommendations for lessening your tax burden? And if you own a business, he should have reviewed those returns as well and had recommendations for lessening your business tax and personal tax burden as well.

Likewise, when was the last time your CPA reviewed your wealth plan? Did she know what she was looking at? Did she have recommendations for restructuring the plan to minimize your taxes, maximize your return and reduce your risk? Did she comment on anything other than the return you were receiving on your investments?

What I typically find is that the answer is neither the financial advisor nor the CPA has reviewed these documents. And if they did, they did not have any meaningful recommendations.

We haven't even discussed the other members of your financial team. Your attorney, your banker and your insurance agent. Have any of them reviewed any of the related documents from the other advisors and had meaningful comments or recommendations?

Have any of your financial team ever discussed your wealth plan with you much less helped you monitor your progress?

I am sure none of them have done an in-depth analysis of the tax implications of these plans, services and documents. Most CPAs can tell you with complete accuracy what you earned last year and how much you paid in tax on those earnings. A few will give you guidance on how you could have lowered **last** year's taxes. But few have enough knowledge about all aspects of your financial life to give you truly good advice on how all of this ties together and how to truly minimize your taxes, maximize your wealth and minimize your risk.

All of these services and products must work together to effectively maximize your wealth and minimize your tax bite.

Financial advice does not work that way. Every discipline is separated. The professionals do not talk to each other and when they do, they do not speak the same language. And most actually view the professionals of the other disciplines with suspicion. You, the consumer, are left to try to figure it all out on your own.

There has to be a better way!

There is!

Chapter 5

CAN WE TALK?

I know this is a lot to digest. It may take a couple of readings to fully grasp what is being said here and to realize what you should be receiving.

I know you are also probably thinking, "This all sounds good, but how much does all of this cost?" Most clients who fully implement what is outlined here experience reduced cost in either real dollars or as a percentage of assets from cost savings, reduced taxes, increased revenue, and asset growth.[1]

Be wary of any professional who is captive to one company or firm, or who pitches you products with his firm's name attached. Remember the old saying, "If the only tool you have is a hammer everything looks like a nail." As a matter of fact, you should only deal with a professional to whom the product or vehicle selected is a single tool or a combination of tools in a tool chest full of options. In other words, the product employed should not be the focus of the professional's advice.

Who is the ideal candidate for this opportunity?

Our ideal client owns a service business, a professional firm or practice, or is highly compensated. They are typically businesses with gross revenue of $1,000,000 to $10,000,000 and fewer than 50 employees.

Personal taxable income should be $250,000 and you should have $500,000 in invested assets (inclusive of 401(k) or other business benefit plans).

---

1 Per review conducted on March 15, 2014.

If you fit this profile, we would love to talk to you. We are very selective as to who we take on as a client as we only accept four new clients a month.

We will not take on a client if we do not feel we can change their life and get them to their stated goal.

You can contact us at the following:

S. Brooks Wicker, Jr., CPA
4949 Old Brownsboro Rd.
#279
Louisville, KY 40222
Phone: (502) 893-9743 ext. 210
Fax: (502) 893-6963
brooks@wickergroup.com
www.wickergroup.com

APPENDIX

Menu of services:
Contract CFO
Income tax preparation and planning – Global Tax Planning
Outsourced accounting/finance – family office services
Investment management
Benefits planning
Comprehensive financial products and insurance products
Wealth Plan Development and Review
Coordination of:
    Legal services
    Banking
    IT Services
    HR
    Business concierge
    Travel
    Asset acquisition and financing

ABOUT THE AUTHOR

S. Brooks Wicker Jr., CPA, founded Wicker Strategic Wealthcare Group in 1994. A graduate of the University of Kentucky who passed his CPA exam on his first attempt, Wicker has served as a controller and chief financial officer in multiple industries.

Since founding Wicker Strategic Wealthcare, he's worked with clients in Kentucky, Tennessee, Florida, Indiana, and Georgia, helping business owners, professionals, and executives maximize their wealth potential. Wicker Strategic Wealthcare understands that taxation is the greatest deterrent to wealth creation, and the firm focuses on income tax planning as an integral part of any financial plan.

In 2012, Wicker was the Republican nominee to the U.S. House of Representatives for Kentucky's Third Congressional District. He's been married to his wife, Lynda, for more than thirty years, and they reside in Louisville, Kentucky.

PRAISE FOR BROOKS WICKER

I have always been very happy with the level of service provided by Brooks and Wicker Strategic Wealthcare Group. First and foremost, I have always found Brooks to be very responsive, often responding to a telephone call or an email within an hour or two. I have been especially impressed that Brooks maintains this level of responsiveness during periods when I know most accountants are especially busy.

I have been equally impressed with Brooks' competence and knowledge of accounting and tax issues. In addition, he possesses the unique ability to simplify accounting, financial and tax concepts and clearly communicate the essential information to the financial lay person such as myself.

David D.
Louisville, KY

Ten years ago we started with a small two man operation.

We needed an accountant and chose Wicker Strategic Wealthcare Group.

With the assistance, guidance and sound fiscal advice of Wicker Strategic Wealthcare Group (Brooks Wicker) we have grown into a multi-million dollar business and now employ over 20 people.

Wicker Strategic Wealthcare Group is the height of professionalism, having helped to bring us where we are today. They are dependable, trustworthy, and always deliver on time as promised. Brooks has never in ten years been too busy to assist and guide us through the tough and growth times.

It will suffice to say Wicker Strategic Wealthcare Group is our choice and will remain our choice as long as we are in business.

Neil J.
Louisville, KY

Brooks is a very strong technical accountant that is focused on the bottom line for his clients. He brings personality, care and sincerity to his clients.

Steve Angel
Louisville, KY

When it comes to financial decisions Brooks is the go to person. Even though we live hours apart Brooks is as close as your telephone. He guides you through decision making processes that you can take to the bank.

Kyle Dunn
Eddyville, KY

Nearly twenty years ago, in the midst of tax season, I had the good fortune of contacting Brooks Wicker to do my personal taxes. At the time this was nothing more than an urgent need with no expectation of a lasting relationship.

Twenty years later, this happy accident has developed into a lasting and profoundly trusting relationship. So much so that I have confidently and proudly recommended a number of other close friends to Brooks. It is no surprise that they too have come to rely upon Brooks for his dependable guidance and comprehensive management of their long-term wealth creation.

Brooks has never sought to sell me anything, but drawing upon a wide array of options and deep professional experience and knowledge, he has always developed optimum solutions tailored to my individual objectives.

Albert Woodington, III
Louisville, KY

We hired Brooks Wicker and Wicker Strategic Wealthcare Group three years ago and what a difference. We now have a CFO not just an accounting firm where you are just another client.

We meet with Brooks at least monthly to review where we are on our goals and benchmarks. Now that we understand the leverage points that Brooks taught us about, we are growing the value and profitability of our firm and we are seeing outstanding results. The value of our firm has grown by 55 % in just three short years and we are looking forward to continued growth.

Brooks and Wicker Strategic Wealthcare Group have helped me substantially increase my wealth and plan how to keep it and pass it along. I highly recommend Wicker Strategic Wealthcare Group to any business owner who is truly serious about developing multigenerational wealth.

John T. McCarthy, III
Louisville, KY

www.ingramcontent.com/pod-product-compliance
Lightning Source LLC
Chambersburg PA
CBHW051302170526
45165CB00004B/1815